WORKSHOPS
THAT
MATTER

How to Plan and Run
Relevant, Productive and
Memorable Workshops

WORKSHOPS THAT MATTER

How to Plan and Run Relevant,

Productive and Memorable Workshops

Copyright © 2017 by George Zelina

WORKSHOPS
THAT
MATTER

How to Plan and Run
Relevant, Productive and
Memorable Workshops

GEORGE ZELINA

I hear and I forget.

I see and I remember.

I do and I understand.

~ Confucius

To Szabolcs Kéri

I learned from the best. Thank you!

TABLE OF CONTENTS

FOREWORD

work•shop

(ˈwɜrkˌʃɒp)

n.

a seminar or small group that meets to explore some subject, develop a skill or technique, carry out a creative project, etc.

It is my firm belief that running a successful workshop is one of the most exciting and uplifting experiences a person can have. When I'm running a workshop I look around and see all the satisfied and happy faces and I know that everyone is taking something positive away with them. It is a win-win for everyone. Provided, of course, that I do it right.

It is also a great career. I love knowing that I am helping people in their work and assisting the businesses that employ them. Running a workshop puts me in that rare state of mind called "flow state," where I become the experience. It becomes impossible to separate myself as a person performing an action from the action itself. At the risk of sounding a little kooky, when I'm running a workshop, responding to the subtle changes in the environment, and feeding off the energy of the participants, I feel at one with myself. The feeling is so dynamic and so all encompassing, the time flies when I'm running them.

I have participated and facilitated many workshops and I can tell you, doing it right requires commitment, humbleness and the ability to react quickly. This book is for anyone who is interested in facilitating workshops and/or brainstorming sessions, or anyone who is just curious how interactivity and games help individuals leave their comfort zones and come up with ideas out of the box.

We all have creative minds. We all have the answers we need, but sometimes we have to step out from our usual, everyday work environments and do something different, do something memorable.

Come with me and I will show you how.

WHY WORKSHOPS WORK

One of the most important skills a workshop facilitator can have is the ability to put themselves in the shoes of both the client and the group being taught. That way, you, as facilitator, better understand the task at hand, and the issues facing your group as they move towards achieving their goal.

So in this, the first chapter, we shall do just that. In later chapters we'll move on to the practical activities and skills that are needed. But first, let's look at why a business leader might want to hold workshops.

We will step into their shoes.

It doesn't matter whether you are Google, Microsoft, Forbes or the little business on the street corner.

If you allow your company to stand still, then it goes backwards. As Albert Einstein explained in his Theory of Relativity, motion is relevant to your starting position.

If you stand still, and the rest of the world keeps moving, then relative to them you are going backwards. And no business wants that.

But if most of us agree with that idea as a concept, it begs the question – how do we make our business move forward?

And what exactly does moving a business forward mean? Surely, some of the goals we would seek to achieve in doing this would include the following:

- Improving the performance of your workforce
- Learning and implementing the best practices in your field
- Developing unity in your workforce, so that they are all aware of the common goal, and are committed to achieving it
- Creating a happy working environment

If we all agree this are worthwhile goals, then one of the most powerful ways of moving your company forward is to initiate workshops for you and your team.

Understanding your WHY

Simon Sinek is an expert in the field of motivation and team building. He believes that the starting point for any business's growth and development is to get back to basics. This is the WHY behind the business. In other words, the WHY is the company's key aims and the reason for its existence.

Let's look at how this knowledge translates to action. Once Simon, with a team's assistance, has established the reason for the business, he then helps the workforce take the next step. They know why they work, but now they need to understand the HOW. In other words, they need to know the ways in which the core aims can be achieved.

Only then does the team begin to consider the WHAT – how that initial aim is realized.

Interestingly, Simon does not describe himself as a workshop specialist, but as an innovator and creative thinker.

He passes on his skills to allow businesses to discover the reason behind their ideas, so that their output is the very best that it can be.

This involves workshops on visions and values, design and innovation.

The Outcomes of This Approach

Through following the model established by Simon Sinek, those taking the workshops will develop their understanding of this golden circle of WHY – HOW - WHAT. They will formulate, through their activities, a better understanding of the passion at the core of the business in which they work.

They will learn how to make the 'Why' element real. They will also understand their own workplace in the context of other businesses who have progressed through this model.

Why Workshops?

There are other ways in which businesses can take their company forward. They can shoulder the cost of bringing in outside workers to offer the expertise they feel is lacking. They can send their staff off to off-site training courses, which also costs money.

Or...they can run a workshop, which usually makes better use of their budget.

Another advantage a workshop offers is the sense of unity, of learning together, of understanding core values and of gaining enjoyment in each other's company. And there's a real need for this. I mean, let's face it, we all know of businesses, even small to medium sized ones, where the only time the staff actually gets together for a purpose other than doing their jobs is at the annual Christmas shindig.

And even then, there's not a lot of real interaction. Following the dictates of natural human behaviour, employees tend to congregate in departmental groups. I mean, who would want to spend their evening doing something else besides listening to glory stories of the sales staff winning over stubborn buyers?

Pretty much everybody except the Sales department!

On top of all this, the CEO usually spends the entire duration of these forced mixers desperately trying and failing to integrate the parts of his workforce.

By contrast, in a business where workshops are a part of the culture, the members of the staff are used to working together. A unified company is more productive than an office where each department operates in a vacuum. Solidarity builds success.

What Makes A Successful Workshop?

As we can see, a successful workshop is characterized by as much involvement of the staff team as is possible.

If your business is to gain a coherent approach to its goals, then everybody has to know what those goals are. They also need to know the challenges they will face in achieving them. For instance, the person who answers the phones might not need to know of the difficulties of securing a sale, but if he or she does, then their response to the telephone call from the waiting customer will be more focused and efficient.

A specialist heart surgeon, to employ an analogy, might not need to know everything about podiatry, but a working knowledge of other aspects of medicine can help him or her become more effective in their specific field.

What Can a Good Workshop Help You to Achieve?
There are a number of answers to this question.

The point covered above, which is that it is useful to know as much about the company as a whole as possible, links back to Simon Sinek's point about understanding the 'Why' behind a strategy.

By sharing the entire expertise of your team, you are opening the floor to different ways of thinking. And different ways of thinking are what lead to solutions. Your sales staff might be struggling with the time spent uploading their sales information. But the answer might come from your technician who, not having known of the problem, immediately suggests the simple solution of employing software which allows information to be passed from any location.

Knowledge of the competition is crucial to a successful business. By workshopping, more staff are collected together to answer the question, therefore multiplying the possible ways of solving the problem. It might be as simple as overhearing a guest at a dinner party share a positive experience that they had with a rival company. This is another opportunity to learn. The indirect benefit of community spirit is a huge plus that can come from holding workshops. There is little that offers more benefit to productivity than a happy workforce. If more friendships are developed, because there are more people to get to know, then that spirit is deepened and enhanced.

In this chapter, we have looked at why workshops are important and the benefits they can bring to your business. In the next chapter, we will look at what makes a brilliant workshop facilitator.

What Makes a Brilliant Workshop Facilitator

Think back to the best teachers of your school or college days. It is extremely likely that they held a few common characteristics.

If you think about it, your favourite teacher probably enjoyed what they taught, they probably exerted control, but not overtly. They just conveyed that they were 'in charge.' And, usually the best teachers let you learn things yourself – they did not lecture, but somehow, at the end of the lesson, you knew more than at the beginning.

The best teachers possess the same skills as the best facilitators. In fact, the two words should be synonymous with each other.

What follows, then, are the skills that anyone who wants to be a great facilitator will need to learn.

The Ability To Listen

Whether you are a professional facilitator or are seeking to add this talent to your general business skill set, the ability to listen is one of the most important things you will need.

Good listening will enable you to get a feel for the group you are working with. Are they keen to learn? Would they rather be somewhere else? Is there a big ego there that will need to be directed? Of course, the ability to listen is not just something you will need in spades, but an important skill to be shared with the group with which you are working.

Planning

A good facilitator will have worked with their client to establish what EXACTLY it is that the group needs to achieve. He or she then goes away and constructs activities which will take the group towards these goals.

Planning includes timing. There are a limited number of hours in the session, and although every group has different dynamics, such as whether they will find themselves throroughly immersed in an activity – or pass through it very quickly – they will still need to achieve the goals of the session. Therefore, the ability to move the session forward, to maintain its energy and pace, is essential.

The skill needed to do this is the ability to plan, so that the facilitator knows when to move the session on.

Flexibility

It is a rare thing indeed for a workshop to run faultlessly through every stage of your planning. Generally speaking, the better you know your group, the more likely it is that you will achieve your goal. But of course, the dynamics of a group on a particular day, and the particular focus of the group, are all subject to change. The need to be flexible, therefore, is tantamount to your workshop's success.

Flexibility is a bit like the internet cloud. It appears to be something mysterious and wonderful, but it is actually quite mundane. And just as the cloud is as ordinary of a set of servers in a warehouse, flexibility is, at base, just detailed preparation.

Having a range of alternative activities which can provide a different direction to a group, or offer them additional ways of dealing with an aspect of their session allows the facilitator to be flexible in their work.

The idea is to implement the changes in direction so seamlessly, that the group won't even notice that they are being directed, or that the objective of an activity has shifted. Ideally, when the workshop is done, the participants will simply look back at the event and think about what a great time they had, blissfully unaware of the changes.

Retain a Sense of Your Own Role

In other words, the best facilitators keep their ego at bay. Instead of drawing the focus of the group to themselves, they create situations where the group can learn. The facilitator merely directs the group's attention to the tasks at hand.

This is called *collaborative learning*. It is where the group takes the lead for their own learning. Collaborative learning is an extremely powerful model, because the group feels in charge of their own achievements. With this method, the learning sticks. Ideas and practices are pulled from the realm of theory and made a part of lived experience. As a result, the process of collaborative learning is enjoyable and the group feels empowered.

The facilitator's job in all of this is simply to offer steering. They make sure the group doesn't stray from their objective and they chip in with the occasional prompt.

Collaborative learning, from the position of the facilitator, doesn't usually come naturally. You have points you wish to deliver, directions you wish your group to take. But the group doesn't always adhere to these lines. Being able to run with the collaborative approach, when you desperately want to simply tell the group what they need to know, takes confidence and practice. But ultimately it is the best way for the group to learn.

Tactful Discipline

One advantage that leading children has over leading adults is that, if the children misbehave, you can always tell them to stop.

You can't do that with adults.

So, a tactful approach to discipline needs to be developed. There are a number of tricks to have in your armory.

For example, dividing your group into small units, even down to pairs, creates an environment where everybody gets the chance to speak, and the discussion is not dominated by one or two individuals.

The confidence to say, with a smile, 'let's move on now' when an argument gets heated, or goes round and round in circles, takes time to develop so that it is delivered in a way that does not cause offense.

It doesn't matter if your group is a selection of senior managers, each of them out to impress the boss, or a nervous group of new interns. As the facilitator, you are the boss.

However, just like with a group of kids, if the session is well planned, the pacing is maintained, and the group is kept busy, discipline problems are far less likely to occur.

Clear Instructions

For the most part, people come to a workshop expecting to learn and expecting to take direction. Indeed, sometimes they can be too complicit and need to be empowered to explore their own ideas.

One crucial thing the facilitator needs to learn is the ability to be clear and concise. Instructions need to be unambiguous. They need to be short, simple to follow, and not be too numerous for an activity. Often, a repeated instruction can help to clarify what you have said. Because, as every experienced workshop runner knows, somebody will get the wrong idea. Take it all in stride.

To summarize, to be an effective facilitator, you need to trust in your students to take the lead with their own learning, but you need to shape and direct their discussions to stay on track. You need to be clear about the end goal. Preparation, planning and flexibility are key skills.

And finally, you need to be very clear and straightforward when introducing activities.

PREPARATION

Preparation is one of the key elements of a successful workshop.

It is a bit like putting on a magic show. The audience, in this case those taking the workshop, are wowed by the illusion because they are unaware of the amount of preparation that has gone in to making the trick work.

As you become more experienced as a facilitator, you will develop a store of activities which you can draw on to make planning easier. But at the outset, it is important that you run through the following stages.

What is the Goal?

Working with the client is key here. They are buying your services, so it is important that you deliver results for them. It is important for you and your business as well, since word of mouth recommendations carry the greatest weight, whether in face to face meetings between business owners or friends, or on social media sites.

It is important to share the goal with the group at the outset. It may be, in some circumstances, that it is the group that defines their specific aims for a session. (In which case, even more preparation is needed, so that you can fulfill their needs.)

Which Milestones Will Be Completed?

These are the steps that you will work on with your group to build their understanding of the final product – that is, their grasp of the goal.

They are useful measures for the following sections of your workshop:

- The Client – he or she can see that you are working to plan, and that his staff is learning the right things. This is an opportunity for you to explain to your client the importance of self-learning and collaboration by the group. After all if he or she were the expert, they would be running the workshop themselves. By definition, your client is very likely to be a successful person, and they may have their own views of what defines success, which could be inappropriate for a workshop setting. For example, you are not delivering a lecture!
- Those Taking the Workshop – to keep your group motivated you need well-paced, entertaining activities. People learn more when they are having fun. But at the same time you are working with professionals in their field. They will want to know that they are progressing towards the goal that is being sought.
- Yourself – it is easy to get side-tracked when you are running a session. Having clear milestones outlined helps you to keep the workshop on track.

Breaking Down Planning

Whether it is a workshop with a pre-defined goal, or one where the goal is defined by the group a well-planned agenda is still important. As is sharing the planning of the session with your group. People get much more out of an event where they can see how they are moving to their goal.

Facilitators who try to wow their clients by leading activities which can seem at first to be unrelated run the risk of losing the interest of their customers long before the final outcome is revealed.

Workshops can run for any length of time. Usually, for businesses, it is most cost effective to hire the facilitator for a minimum of half a day – few Workshop organizers would be keen to work for less than that, as it means that, in most cases, the rest of their day is wasted.

However, they can run for two or even three days.

Depending on the length of time available, the facilitator needs to plan effectively. A long workshop gives more opportunity to explore in depth, but equally activities need to be planned to retain the interest of those taking part.

Planned Examples

We have below agendas for three-day and one-day workshops. As you can see, there is no pre-determined goal for these. Of course, the planning would reflect the specifics of the goal. Even where the group is defining the outcomes they would like, it is still the case that the facilitator will have gained a broad idea of where the session will end up. This will have been gleaned by the business of the client, and by discussions when the sessions are set up.

Three Day Workshop General Outline

Day 1	Day 2	Day 3
10:00-10:30 Kick-off	10:00-10:30 Brainstorming game	10:00-10:30 Team building game
10:30-11:00 Icebreaker game	10:30-11:30 Presentation of the 2nd topic	10:30-11:00 2 teams forming on topic 5 & 6
11:00-12:00 Ideas to post-its	11:30-12:00 2 teams forming on topic 3 & 4	11:00-12:00 Small team works on topic 5 & 6

12:00-1:00 Lunch	12:00-1:00 Lunch	12:00-1:00 Lunch
1:00-1:30 Energetic game	1:00-1:30 Energetic game	1:00-1:30 Energetic game
1:30-2:30 Categorization of post-its into topics, prioritization, 2 teams forming	1:30-2:30 Small team works on topic 3 & 4	1:30-2:30 Presentation of the 5th topic
2:30-3:00 Break, game	2:30-3:00 Break, game	2:30-3:00 Break, game
3:00-4:00 Small team works on Top 2 topics	3:00-4:00 Presentation of the 3rd topic	3:00-4:00 Presentation of the 6th topic
4:00-4:30 Break, game	4:00-4:30 Break, game	4:00-4:30 Break, game
4:30-5:30 Presentation of the 1st topic	4:30-5:30 Presentation of the 4th topic	4:30-5:30 Summary of the workshop, next steps, follow-up
5:30-5:45 Wrap-up of the day, feedback cycle	5:30-5:45 Wrap-up of the day, feedback cycle	5:30-5:45 Wrap-up of the workshop, feedback cycle

One Day Workshop General Outline

Day 1
10:00-11:00 Kick-off, discuss the 2 topics to cover on the workshop
11:00-11:30 Icebreaker game
11:30-12:00 Find owners for the 2 topics and form small groups
12:00-1:00 Lunch
1:00-1:30 Energetic game
1:30-2:30 Small team works on the 2 topics
2:30-3:00 Break, game
3:00-4:00 Presentation of the 1st topic
4:00-4:30 Break, game

4:30-5:30 Presentation of the 2nd topic
5:30-5:45 Summary of the workshop, next steps, follow-up
5:45-6:00 Wrap-up, feedback cycle

As you can see, there is a real emphasis on enjoyable, fun activities. And they are broken into small, manageable chunks. The importance of pace and fun cannot be over-estimated.

STARTING OFF

The first ten minutes of your workshop are the most important. We all know that first impressions can make or break the experience that follows.

The reason real estate agents offer specially brewed coffee at open house events is because they want to make an instant impression – research suggests that a buyer is lost within twenty seconds of entering the property. Get over that, and there is fair chance of a sale.

It is the same with a workshop.

You do have an advantage over your participants, however. Right from a very young age, they have been trained to listen to the teacher. That rarely leaves a person, and they will therefore usually immediately adopt the 'well-behaved student' persona that was drilled into them from their first day at school.

This politely offered attention doesn't last for long, though.

So those first ten minutes are where you set the tone for the sessions ahead.

Don't Talk Too Much

People prefer to *do*, rather than simply listen. So, the facilitator needs to be strict. We all have funny stories and glorious tales of success stored in our brains. But it is the recipient's appreciation of your communications that you are seeking rather than your enjoyment of telling a well-worn tale. For the introductory period, be VERY clear and VERY concise. You'll have plenty of time to tell your jokes and funny stories throughout the rest of the day.

Outline the Purpose of the Workshop

Again, this needs to be short and sweet. At this stage, you are not delivering the goal – that will come in practical sessions later, but you need to let your group know why they are there.

Working Out Your Group

Remember, sitting in front of you will be people with varied preconceptions. Let's take a look at a few:

- *Miss Goody-Goody* – actually, that is a bit unfair because these are the people who are going to make your workshop a success. These are the ones who see the time spent at the workshop as valuable in helping them perform better at their work. They are your instant allies – just beware, strong supporters turn into the strongest opponents if you fail to deliver.

- *Mrs Can I Just Ask…* - this lady is very keen. Her keenness is so stunning, in fact, that she will seek to dominate every discussion, want to be every volunteer. Usually, the group will tolerate her for a bit, but then get fed up. Ultimately, she is on your side. But you will need to keep her busy while politely and tactfully giving others a chance.

- *Mr It's Better Than Work* – this chap is happy to be there, because he feels that it is a day off from work. He is somebody you really have to win over by your work or you will find he becomes a negative non-participant.

- *Madam I Don't Need This* – one of your hardest participants, this lady already knows it all and is aware that there is nothing you can offer that will improve her performance which, she knows, is already quite outstanding.
- *Mr What's The Point?* – the cynic, whose negativity will ruin the day if allowed to spread.
- *Miss Can I Clarify?* – another member of the group very much on your side, but lacking in confidence. She will dominate your session if given the chance, seeking reassurance on points that both she, and everybody else, already understands.
- *Mr Let's Have A Laugh* – unless he's really annoying, and nobody finds him funny, the joker in the pack can become a great ally, keeping good humour up and being prepared to be the subject as well as a constant supplier of laughs.

Whether they are on your side or not, they all still deserve your best attention, and it is one of the skills of the facilitator to work out how to be as inclusive as possible.

Lay Down The Rules

Remember, your group has been through school, and are therefore used to the leader of the group (that is how the facilitator will be regarded) setting the rules.

By being clear – in a polite, concise and reasoned way, your group is much more likely to follow the rules of the day.

What Are The Rules?

Number One – Establish an atmosphere of complete openness

(This will be confirmed by the person who hired you at the outset)

The rule is that what happens in the workshop stays in the workshop.

If you cannot have an atmosphere where participants feel confident and safe to be honest, then the outcomes everybody seeks will be compromised.

Number Two – It's not about winning arguments

It is important for everyone to know that the workshop is not an arena for scoring points or winning arguments. As with all the rules, this should be presented in a polite and friendly way, but is crucial if all participants are to feel involved.

Number Three – Respect

Emphasize that within the workshop everybody is equal, from the CEO to the cleaning staff. Everybody's views will be listened to and considered carefully, and everybody will get the chance to say what they wish to say. Again, this is all about ensuring inclusivity for every participant.

Number Four – Stay On Task

Of course, the most important subject of this rule is you, the facilitator. If your sessions are inspiring, well organized and efficient, then the participants will stay on task. However, it is still important to make the point.

Everybody needs to know that they are still at work, even if it is a different sort of work than they're used to.

Number Five – No Phones, Laptops, Tablets, Gadgets and E-book Readers

Many people are embarrassed about giving instructions to adults, but as I keep emphasizing, the participants do tend to do as they are told. You can't force them to turn off their phone, but can request it. It's worth nothing that while you can't put those who won't turn off their phones in the corner with dunce caps on their head, not too many people will content you on this issue. After all, it takes a very blatant person to ruin a session by overtly using their phone, or not to respond to peer pressure by the other members of the group who are there to learn.

Having run through the first ten minutes of your workshop, in the next chapter we will consider the use of effective ice-breakers, both for groups of strangers and for people who are already used to working together.

ICE BREAKERS

Your workshop should properly start with some ice breakers. People's natural reserve can create reluctance to participate in a new activity. This is natural. The general tension of a new and unfamiliar arrangement can be broken with some fun activities. The idea is to engage the participants' minds and stoke their enthusiasm.

It doesn't matter whether or not you are working with a group who know each other or not, the ice-breaker activities will remove anxieties and encourage ever greater participation.

However, the content of the ice breaker will vary depending on how familiar your group members are with each other.

Five Ice Breakers for Groups That Know Each Other
You Didn't Know That!
Equipment – sentence starters, pencils

You prepare sheets with sentence starters, such as 'I have never…', 'My favourite time of the day is…'. The sentence starters are given out, and your participants complete the sheet with a few sentences of their own – it shouldn't be too long, especially if you have a larger group. They should try to complete their story with something that is not widely known, but something that they're okay with being shared. When everybody is done, they should put the papers upside down, pick up one random paper and have someone read it aloud. After each one is read, the participants can guess who wrote what.

Guess What Happened

Equipment – a collection of 'events', hat or box

Write a series of events on strips of paper, such as 'I have just won the lottery' or 'It's raining and I forgot my umbrella'. Put the events in the hat or box. Each participant has to draw one of the events from the box and perform the event. You can allow words or not, depending on how confident the group seems. Whoever guesses the event correctly is the next performer.

Scavenger Hunt

Equipment – list of items to scavenge

This is a great activity for people who already know each other a little bit, because some knowledge helps the activity to be completed.

Divide the party into groups of two or three. Give each team the same list of, say, ten things to find. You will need to set the limits of the search area, but it works even better when the group are in their home surroundings. Items to find could include 'a group photo in front of something yellow', 'the funniest thing you can find' or 'something which looks like an aligator.' They have 20 minutes to collect all and at the end they present what they've found. Participants can vote for the best items.

Toilet Revelations

Equipment – roll of toilet paper

This is a fun game. Pass around a roll of toilet paper and say that people can take as many strips as they like, as long as there is enough to go around.

Once everybody has their selection, then your reveal that for each sheet of paper, the holder must tell one thing about themselves that the others do not know.

Question and Answer Madness
Equipment – Two cards, such as index cards or plain postcards, for each participant

This game gets the workshop off with a laugh. On half of the cards write questions. You can devise your own along the style of those below. Then, with the other half, you write answers.

One person picks a card and reads the question, then the next takes an answer and reads that. Go until you are out of cards.

Example questions:
1) Would you like to be a millionaire?
2) Do you visit restaurants often?
3) Do you enjoy your work?
4) Do you wear a wig?
5) Do you enjoy music?
6) Would you like to sit next to me?
7) Do you love me?
8) Are you modest?
9) Can I rely on you?
10) Do you make friends easily?

Example answers:

1) No, I tried once, but it was a disaster.
2) It is my life's ambition.
3) No, I come from a good background.
4) I can tell you in private.
5) I must plead the 5th amendment.
6) Only in bed.
7) On payday.
8) When I am bored.
9) I try not to talk about it.
10) I'll try it if you will.

You can see the idea.

Five Ice Breakers for Strangers
It's On My Resume

Equipment – question slips, pencils

For this game, prepare a number of questions on slips. They should be simple questions such as 'Have you ever been in the front row at a concert?' or 'Have you ever cooked a sit-down meal for ten or more people?'

The slips and pencils are given out, and the workshop members ask the simple questions. When they get a 'Yes', the person signs their name under the question.

Protect The Egg

Equipment – sticky tape, scissors, straw, paper clips etc. One egg per group plus a couple of spares (in case of accident)

Divide the group into teams of three to five. As much as is possible, avoid having people who normally work together joining together in a group. You want the groups to be comprised of people who do not know each other well. Give each group a certain time in which they need to design a contraption to catch their egg when it is dropped from a given height. After a set period of time, test each contraption. Applaud the winning team.

Patchwork

Equipment – whiteboard, pens.

Draw a matrix of all participants' names both horizontally and vertically. Ask them to start conversations with everyone else about their interests, hobbies. Once they find one common interest, both of them draws down a symbol in his box which reminds them about that. If there are ten people, give them 20 minutes to finish this game, reminding them about the time as you go. At the end everyone gets the best workshop souvenir ever. Some people printed out the pictures we took about the drawings. This game is my definition of ice breaker.

Superlatives

No equipment needed.

This is an excellent team game ice breaker, as your participants need to communicate with each other.

Divide your group into teams of six to eight people (ten maximum). Then, issue an instruction which the group must follow. Examples can include 'birthdates from the beginning to the end of the year' or, 'shortest to furthest distance from the home of the workshop.' Give them a maximum of ten examples.

What is It?

Equipment – lots of objects with one syllable names, such as a pen, a knife, a card etc.

The group stands in a circle. Person one chooses an object and says to person two: 'This is a (fork)'; person two replies 'A what?'; person one 'A fork' and person two 'Oh a fork'.

Person two then carries out the same conversation with person three, while person one starts the conversation with a new object. Person two is therefore having to conduct two conversations simultaneously. The game continues until every object has made its way round the complete circle.

There are many other ice breakers, and over time you will find that you develop your own variants, as you discover what works and what is less reliable. Most of the ice breakers are interchangeable between groups that know each other and those that are strangers.

But all serve to create the environment in which more serious learning can take place. There is also nothing wrong with inserting an ice breaker if you sense your workshop is starting to lose a little steam.

First Activity

Now it is time to start the meat of your workshop. You have already laid down the rules and broken the ice. Everybody is enthusiastic and keen to get started.

Even the potentially tricky members of your group are ready to go.

Here is how we proceed, depending on whether or not the workshop has a pre-defined topic.

Where Topics Are <u>Not</u> Pre-Defined
Here, the challenge is to get the group unified on what they wish their workshop to be about. In this situation, each member is going to have their own area of interest, their own concerns they wish to be addressed, even occasionally their own agendas.

The session probably doesn't want to become a huge criticism of the management team of the organization.

However, almost certainly when you set up the workshop you will have held discussions with the person in charge. They will have at least given you an idea of what they wish to achieve, albeit within the context of what the group has decided.

Step One – give out post-it notes to everyone, and ask them to write down the issues that are the most important to them within the general theme outlined.

Step Two – get the group to put the post-its onto a whiteboard. Ask them to read the post-its out loud as they put them up. It can be quite chaotic, as people comment on the views of others. As facilitator and therefore leader, this has to be managed. Allow the comments and observations, but reiterate that we will be able to prioritize the list in the next activity.

Step Three – once the whiteboard has every suggestion written down, ask the team to divide them into groups or themes. You may well have discovered that the same issue comes up several times but with different wording. That is fine, in fact, it can be helpful with prioritizing the theme.

Step Four – issue three votes to every member. They can use those votes as they wish. For example, they could allocate all three votes to one of the themes, or split them evenly between three themes. They do not have to vote for their own ideas if others have emerged which they feel are more relevant.

Step Five – the allocation of the votes will help to provide the workshop with a clear list of priorities to address. Explain to the group that quality outweighs quantity, so it is possible that the sessions will not get to cover all of themes.

Where Topics are Pre-defined

In this case, it is always best to be up front. Explain that these topics are the ones the management team have decided upon, and explain why. If participants are aware of the reasons for a topic, they are much more likely to buy in to participation with it.

What Happens Next?

This is where the preparation you have put in pays dividends. If you were lucky enough to know in advance exactly what the focus of your workshop would be, then things are a little easier.

You could plan and prepare in advance, and start your activities so that they address the said topics.

Where the group has decided on the topics themselves, you would have come with a range of activities which could be adapted on a best fit basis which can now be presented to the group.

In either situation, it is worth buying yourself some thinking time. It is important that you are clear what the group wants to achieve, or needs to explore, and consider the best ways of doing this.

However, where the workshop facilitator has the advantage of the lecturer is that it is the group themselves who will be leading their own learning.

Therefore, it is possible to set the groups off on discussion activities where they can begin to investigate the topics in hand. During that time, you can have a few minutes to direct your planning, so that you are giving the group the best opportunity to tackle their topics.

An Example To Illustrate the Above

We will use an example relating to a situation where the group has not been given a predefined topic. (In the other case, where a topic is in place, then you would go from the point at which the topic has been decided upon by the group.)

The management, in our example, has given the very broad theme of wanting the workforce to be able to contribute more to the company's success.

You hand out the post-its tactfully, to ensure that the group doesn't feel that they are being criticized, you ask them to write down ways in which they feel they contribute to the firm's success, and ways in which they could do more.

You collect in the ideas, and write down the ones in which people feel they could offer more. These may often take the form of participants identifying barriers, such as inadequate technology, to their ability to contribute.

The vote takes place. Your group is now in all likelihood very engaged. They have had their ice breaker, and they can see that the session is going to be productive, and address very real issues.

You now have your topics in a priority order. Let's say that the topics are: poor communication first, lack of technology second, and uncertainty on the company's main objectives third. (This is the point in the workshop where an already agreed-upon theme would come in.) Depending on the size of your group, you might divide them into two or three different groups to tackle the first two or three items on the list. It is always best to keep groups to a manageable size, say three to six. If they get any bigger, then the quieter or less confident people can drop out of the discussions and leave it to others.

At this stage, you will set these groups off for a short period, perhaps an hour, to discuss and get their heads around the topics they will be addressing. You will use that time to fine tune your planning, and make sure that you visit each group at least once, ideally twice, to ensure that they are on track and can have any questions addressed.

SMALL GROUP ACTIVITIES

In this chapter, we will look at how small group activities can be used to help to fulfill a workshop's aims.

More specifically, we will consider how a small group activity is best structured. And finally we'll look at some examples that can be adapted to fit this method.

Over-Riding Principles

By now, your workshop is well underway. The goals have been identified, and all of the warm up ice breakers have been completed. Everone knows each other and teams have been formed.

At this point your participants are ready and eager to get into the nitty and gritty of solving the issues, achieving the goals as identified by either yourself (through your discussions with the management of the business that has hired you) or through the groups themselves.

The small group activities are designed to tackle these goals, with each group looking at either a complete goal or an aspect of a goal in a way that will alter enable them to report back to the rest of the group.

The extent of the work that they need to do, whether it is a detailed examination of a small aspect of a goal, or a goal itself in broader terms, will depend on the size of the group itself.

Step One – Sort Groups Sizes

For small group activities, an ideal group size is three to four participants. This gives enough for the group to bounce ideas off of each other, but is not so large that some members are able to withdraw from participation, either through choice or because they are intimidated by the large numbers discussion.

The number of goals and aspects of goals to cover will be determined by the group size. Each group will take one theme. Ask for people to take ownership of the various categories. Most often, most subjects will attract interest, and you may have to make decisions as to who will lead each group.

However, reassure that *everyone* will get the chance later in the workshop to take the lead.

Get the leaders to pick their groups – try to ensure that this is light-hearted and not competitive – you don't want the last people to be selected to feel alienated. Then set the groups off with their task.

Step Two – Getting To Work

You will need to make sure that each group has something to write on and with. By far the best way is to issue whiteboards or flipcharts and marker pens, since these are easy to edit on and the writing is big enough for the whole group to see easily.

They will need to undertake the following tasks. In each, they should discuss the issue and reach a conclusion. They will later be reporting back to the remainder of the group, so their conclusions should be clear and concise.

The tasks are:

- To define the aspect or goal they have been given. They must articulate exactly what it is they are looking to solve. If they are unsure, they should ask you or other people.

- To consider possible solutions to the problem. Again, discussion and agreement should be reached for the ways that they will tackle the issues.

- To identify milestones and deadlines. Here, they will identify the stages to go through to reach their solutions. These should be identified as clear milestones, with deadlines set with hard times by which they should be met. Defining owners for each actionable is also helpful.

Step Three – Final Actions

The final task for each group is to get their notes, observations and points in order so that they can be presented to the group for discussion. As facilitator, you should perhaps emphasize to the group that it is worth spending extra time on this portion of the work, to ensure that their presentation is easily understood by the other participants. This is important, since the other participants have not spent time discussing the issue in detail and are coming to it "green," as it were.

Step Four – Time

Depending on the time allotted for the workshop, the entire goal could be discussed in one session. Or, if the topic of the workshop is fairly complex or wide ranging, two or even three sessions may be needed.

It is really up to you as the facilitator to decide upon the time frame, taking into consideration how many groups are participating, the amount of time available, and the extent of the aims of the workshop.

An Illustrative Example

Let us now consider the above in a practical way. The example which follows can be adapted to different situations.

The Subject

The group we are using is made up of three people considering the use of technology within the company.

Defining the Goal

Here, discussions could lead to the following conclusions. Firstly, that the technology in use at the company entails the sales team reporting back to the company to input their data. This data must then be manually sent to the finance, administration, management and supply teams.

This arrangement is inefficient in that it is both time-consuming and leads to mistakes. It also means that no one group has a comprehensive overview of the entire process.

Looking at Solutions

In our example, the kinds of solutions the group could come up with might include the company investing in cloud based software which allows access from multiple points. This, in theory, would provide better efficiency for the sales staff, as they could input their sales information from anywhere. It could also reduce administration time since all parts of the business could be accessed from their own stations. It could also make an oversight clearer because the management team can now see all aspects of the process – sales, supply, and payment. Finally, it could reduce the risk of error because it reduces the times that the information needs to be inputted.

Milestones and Deadlines

The group might identify the following milestone and deadlines.

- Sell the benefits to the business' leaders to encourage their investment. This could take place at the next monthly meeting for the whole staff.
- Give time for the company to research the best systems. Again, in our example, this is all theoretical, but a decision could be required by the following staff meeting.
- Buying the system and training the staff in its use. This could be set for completion at a key point in the year, such as the beginning of the financial year or after the summer period when holidays have mostly been taken.
- Reviewing the system. The group could recommend, for example, a year to trial the system before deciding on its success.

Preparing to report back

One way for a group to report back the decisions could be for the leader to officially restate the definition of their task.

This person would then return at the end to organize the taking of questions. Another person could be responsible for presenting the solutions. A third person could be in charge of identifying milestones and deadlines.

By delegating the work out, each person has ownership of the group's ideas, and remains involved. Also, by dividing the work, each person has longer to prepare an effective report back.

LARGE GROUP DISCUSSIONS

Holding a large discussion, which will involve all participants in the workshop, is the next stage of running your session.

This is the stage where all the ideas that have come out of the small group activities can be put together to reach conclusions and form action plans.

The Aim of Large Group Discussions

The first step is to establish the aims of the session. The principles behind this should be led by the facilitator, although the actual details will be down to the group to decide.

As the facilitator, you should look to achieve the following with the group:

- The formation of an action plan.
- The action plan will offer ways to solve issues with the goals that the group (or decision makers) have determined.
- It should set milestones and deadlines towards the solving of issues.
- It should identify potential barriers to achieving the laid out goals, and offer solutions to dealing with those barriers.
- Where the decision makers are not a part of the workshop, the group should establish certain persons within the group to put forward and represent their views to the management personnel.

How to Present to the Group

As we saw in the previous chapter, the participants have been split up into small groups to allow different topics and aspects of topics to be investigated. And so now comes the point of reporting back.

Because time is an enemy for all workshops – especially when they go well (which, of course, is the idea) - start with the topic that topped the list, as decided by the group, or by the management teams.

As the reporting back takes place, using either non-speaking members, or if you feel it works better to get alternative views, members of other groups who are currently the 'audience,' and put these people into different characters.

The 'hats' these participants wear are meant to represent the different stakeholders involved with the topic.

These could include managers and the CEO, other workers in the company, shareholders, customers, competitors, families of workers – indeed, a brief discussion with the workshop members can help to identify other stakeholders who might not immediately come to mind.

Allow the group to present and discuss, formulating ideas and techniques as they go along. Your role as facilitator here is simply to keep the group on task, and to move things forward if they start to drag on or to repeat. You may choose to act as a scribe, so that all the other participants can concentrate on making contributions.

If you do act as scribe, remind the group if necessary that it is the reporting group who are leading this part of the workshop. You can delegate leadership roles as you see fit. This will help to ensure that the group stays on topic.

Above all else, remember that at the end of the discussions the group is to have satisfied the aim outlined at the outset of this chapter.

Another Approach – Six Thinking Hats

This workshop tool is based on the theories of Edward De Bono, the lateral thinking guru, author, inventor and consultant. This approach can help the group to think out of the box, and by doing so come up with creative ideas which might not otherwise come to mind.

To give the theory some context, it has been successfully used in strategic planning activities by such major international companies as NASA, Shell, Siemens and IBM.

This activity uses actual hats. The hats can be used, depending on the size of the group, with one person wearing multiple hats or many wearing one hat each.

The hats are color coded – so it is possible to literally supply the participant with hats, or even colored badges or stickers. Doing so can help everybody remain clear of the focus of that particular hat wearer.

The White Hat is for Information

Participants wearing the white hats are completely objective. They cannot consider feelings or their personal viewpoint. They also should not consider the viewpoints of others. They are simply interested in data.

Questions White Hat wearers might ask include:
- What data do we hold on this issue?
- Does the data support our views?
- What do we do to find out more?

The Red Hat is for Emotion

Red hat wearers are interested in gut reactions. Because businesses deal with real people, both as workers and customers, emotions are a crucial part of their success. The Red Hat wearers can be very effective in generating enthusiasm for a project.

They might ask questions such as:
- What is my immediate reaction to the project/proposal?
- Why do I feel like this?

The Black Hat is for Discernment

Here, participants are looking to represent caution. They will aim to put the negatives, raise doubts and identify weaknesses in proposals. They can encourage others who have worries to voice them, rather than think that they are the only one with concerns.

It is always best to address worries at the outset of a project, because it can save time later, and a lot of anxiety on the part of participants in a project who might have doubts. Encouraging participants to discuss any doubts they might have frees up the group to think more freely. They know they're in a place where their input is valued. And even though it's best if doubts are discussed early on, be accomodating if they are raised later in the workshop. Consider these raised issues as challenges to better test your ability to be flexible.

Black Hat questions include the likes of:

- Are there potential conflicts here?
- Has anything been overlooked?
- Does anything appear to be unrealistic?

The Yellow Hat is for Optimism.

Yay. Let's go for it! The joyful yellow hat looks to identify reasons to go ahead. It looks to seek solutions not problems, opportunities not difficulties. Yellow Hat wearers seek to generate enthusiasm amongst the participating group on the project.

Yellow questions might be:

- What excites me about this project?
- What might it let us achieve?
- OK, there are some potential problems. Do they really matter?

The Green Hat is for Creativity

Green hat wearers ask questions to get the group thinking out of the box. It represents provocation and investigation.

Questions might include:

- What happens if the budget runs out?
- How are we going to achieve our goals?
- Might other areas of our business be influenced by this project?

The Blue Hat is for Control

This final hat is perhaps the most important. It determines which hat should present at which times and for how long to lead the project to its greatest chance for success.

It might pose such ideas as:

- Which hat next?
- How long for?
- Do we need all the hats?

Do remember, as facilitator, to stress to your workshop that when wearing the hats, members can only operate under the hats' conditions.

When There is No Agreement

- Put the same amount of chairs as the number of members next to each other
- Put the same amount of chairs facing the previous chairs
- Ask the people to sit down and start the debate
- When someone has the same opinion as the current speaker, he should sit in the speaker's row
- When someone has a different opinion as the current speaker, he should sit in the other row facing him
- During the debate, whoever changes his mind, should sit in the other row
- They do it until everyone is in the same row, which means they are all on the same page

The visualization of a debate lets everyone know to have an opinion as they have to choose sides. It also shows the changing or stagnating balance of opposite opinions. Based on my experience, this approach helps people to get on the same page.

Final Section

The final part of working with large discussions is to get as far down the list of topics and aspects of topics as time will allow.

BREAKS, ENERGETIC AND OUT OF THE BOX GAMES

It is a good idea to factor in games and breaks into your programme. Certainly, after ninety minutes of hard, workshop activities a bit of fresh air and a change of scenery will be appreciated. But games also help keep a workshop fresh and lively.

Advantages of Games Breaks

Games can offer the following to your workshop:

- They help the group to remain bonded, with lots of social interaction.
- They get the mind thinking in different, including lateral, ways. This can really help with creating ideas to solve a seemingly intractable problem.
- They help productivity – groups tend to come out of games refreshed and ready for the next piece of 'work'.
- A good game will re-invigorate the group, re-energizing it for the next part of the session.

Oh, and they're also a lot of fun.

Here are some examples of the games that can be used to enliven and refresh a workshop.

Drawing in the Dark

Aim – to be the group that gets the best drawing.

Equipment – one paper per group, pens, objects to draw.

Additional Benefits – communication and creative thinking.

How the Game Works

Divide the group into teams of two. Each team appoints an 'artist'. Each artist sits down to a table with an empty paper and a pen.

The other team member is shown an object by the facilitator. He or she must then describe the object to his or her artist. He or she cannot identify the object and the artist cannot ask questions.

A time limit is set. To keep the game active, keep the time limit short, five minutes is a good amount.

The game is excellent for developing communication skills. The information passed must be clear and concise since it is the only information the artist can glean.

Play the game at least twice, as groups will gain a lot of learning from the errors they make on the first run.

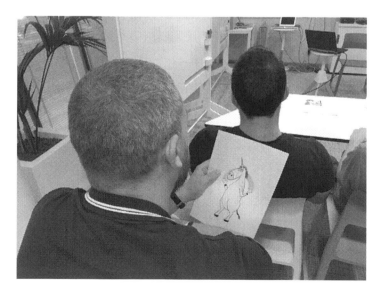

Architects

This is a variation on the Drawing in the Dark game. And, like that game, it is excellent for developing communications skills.

Aim – to be the group that completes the model first, without any mistakes.

Equipment – each group needs two identical sets of 10 to 12 building bricks, such as Lego bricks. By identical, we mean just that. Not only should the size of the sets of bricks be identical, but also the color of each brick.

Additional Benefits – communication skills have to be very precise, as do interpretation skills.

How the Game Works

Teams need to be of at least four people, and no more than eight. Each person has a single role, but two people can take each role in larger groups.

Person A is the architect. He or she creates any kind of shape from the collection of bricks. This person can only speak with Person B, and is not allowed to see what the other members of their team are creating.

Person B is the first communicator. This person can see the architect's design, and speaks to Person C. However, they also cannot see the final product.

Person C is the second communicator. They are allowed to speak with Person B, but not see the architect's design. However, they can see the builder's copy.

Person D is the builder. They must take instruction from Person C and build an EXACT copy, including brick size and color, from Person C. They are not allowed to speak to Person B, or see the architect's original design.

Give around 10 minutes for the activity, and then see which team is the closest. Again, it is worth playing the game twice, so that the lessons learned in the first go-round can be applied on the second try.

A Knotty Problem
Aim – a group aim, to unravel the knot.
Equipment – none, just a reasonably sized space.
Additional Benefits – collaborative work and leadership, time management and communication.

How the Game Works
At least four and up to twelve people can take part. (Larger groups can have two games happening simultaneously, and a competitive element can then be added as groups seek to be the first to finish.)

The group stands in a circle and each raise their right hand. They must grab the raised hand of another person in the group. This is then repeated with the left hand, but the hand grabbed must be of a different person.

The team members must now untangle themselves without breaking the chain of hands that they have created. If the chain breaks, then they must start again, learning the lessons from the previous time. Abstract thinkers come to the fore in games like this, which work best with a time limit provided.

Black Stories

This is a commercial game that works extremely well with groups. It is very exciting, as it features solving a murder, and can involve any number of players.

Aim – to identify the cause of death in a game.

Equipment – Black Stories game pack.

Additional Benefits – Logical thinking, teamwork and communication.

How the Game Works

A player is nominated as 'Game Master'. He or she draws a card and reads the text on the front of the card to everybody else.

They then read the information on the back of the card to themselves.

The rest of the group formulate questions to which the Game Master may ONLY answer YES, NO or, IRRELEVANT, and then only if the question might take the group along the wrong path. If any question is posed which cannot be answered with one of these three words, then the question must be re-phrased.

When the group has solved the cause of death, the game continues with a new Game Master.

Lost at Sea

This is a game where each member has to argue for which items to save from a slowly sinking yacht, and assign each item a rank of importance in priority.

Aim – to get on the same page (and survive).

Equipment – http://insight.typepad.co.uk/lost_at_sea.pdf , print out Page 3 for all participants

Additional Benefits – Logical thinking, teamwork and communication.

How the Game Works

All the instructions and the solution is in the pdf seen above.

Bang!

This game helps the team get focused. It is a drinking game originally but it also works well in workshops.

Aim – to focus on what number comes next.

Equipment – nothing

Additional Benefits – some decent laughs, good substitute for caffeine

How the Game Works

Ask the participants to sit in circle.

They keep counting from 1 but no one can say numbers with a 7 in it (7, 17, 27, etc.) or any number that is a multiple of 7 (7, 14, 21, etc.). Instead they say BANG!

Then play continues to the person who was before the person saying BANG! (so the direction of the circle reverses).

If someone says a number wrong or one of those mentioned above, the game restarts.

My groups usually go until 27, 28… I mean BANG, BANG!

The Internet is full of great team building games. Be brave and try them all out. You can't go wrong with games.

ACT, REACT AND ADJUST

A skill that the best facilitators quickly acquire is to read their participants. Things can appear to be going well, with lively discussions and lots of laughs. Then suddenly, everything changes. The pace starts to slack, people stop contributing and start looking at their watches, or, even worse, chatting among themselves.

How can this happen, when everything was going so well?

A skilled facilitator will be able to pick up on the disatisfaction. Was the laughter coming from everybody, or was it a small group? Were contributions coming from all parts of the room, or was it just the voices of a few that were dominating?

It is the skill of identifying when things start to go off track that sets apart the best workshop leaders.

What are the signs?

Facilitators should constantly be watching and assessing their group's participation. These are the kinds of questions they should be asking themselves, assessing the answers in their observations:

- Am I talking too much?
- Am I watching every person?
- Are there any individuals who look bored, or who have lost focus?
- Who is doing the talking?

- Are a small group dominating the session?
- Is the subject matter under discussion relevant to the task in hand?

These are on-going questions which the facilitator needs to think about regularly.

Prevention is Better than Cure

Much better than dealing with losing some of your group is to ensure that your workshop uses the best learning strategies to keep the participants engaged.

Whatever the activity, there are certain conditions that will aid learning.

Active Learning vs Passive Learning

People enjoy *active* learning more than *passive* learning. Active learning involves the subject involving themselves fully in the activity. This could be by taking part in a discussion, by undertaking a task or involving themselves in a game.

Passive learning is where the subject is not fully engaged. So, a person attending a lecture is learning passively, just taking the information in. They are absorbing without contributing.

The Active Passive model is a continuum, for example, seeing and hearing a video is more active than reading the words, but not as active as designing their own content and making their own video.

There is a pyramid of learning. The strongest way to learn, which is the foundation of the pyramid, involves *doing*, such as taking part in a role play.

The next best way, which is also very good, is to take part in a discussion, or to be the person giving a talk.

The third way, which is still an okay way to learn for the most part, is to both see and hear. For example, watching a role play.

A weak way of learning is simply to look at pictures, or visual aids, and the worst way of all is to listen to somebody else speaking.

It takes a phenomenal interest of the subject, and an excellent speaker, to pass on knowledge using this method. And, of course, it is a LECTURE rather than a WORKSHOP.

The Words Of Confucius

As simple as it seems, applying the words of the great Chinese philosopher will help to make sure your group remain active participants, and therefore learn the most and stay engaged.

The words are simple to learn:
I HEAR and I FORGET
I SEE and I REMEMBER
I DO and I UNDERSTAND.

Keep your group active, and they will understand their learning. It is why rote learning of, say, spelling is not a particularly effective way of learning to spell. Students remember for the test, but then instantly forget it when it comes to their everyday writing.

How To Step In If Necessary

Sometimes, rather like a school teacher, it is necessary to step in and regain the interest of the participants who are losing focus, and get them back on track.

As important as this is, however, it needs to be done tactfully.

Dealing With Mr Know It All

Sometimes people will want to dominate every discussion, feeling that their knowlegde is superior or that they been first to grasp the point. This can be merely enthusiasm, which is great, or it can become boastful, which can be annoying to the participants who are getting crowded out. A good way of dealing with this is to say overtly that you will spend the next session listening to those who have said least. Openness is always best!

The Problem of Miss Nobody Listens To Me

Sometimes, people will keep bringing up the same point, or return to aspects that have already been dealt with.

This can be because they feel that their point has not been listened to. The answer is to actively listen, nodding and affirming points. You do not have to agree with them, and you may need to point out factual errors, but by recapping their point, they will often feel satisfied and happy then for the workshop to progress.

The Eternal and On-Going Problem Associated With Mrs I Know What I Want To Say But I Am Unable To Be Concise.

Sadly, some people do find it difficult to make a concise point. That doesn't mean that they have any less of a right to offer a viewpoint. Let them speak, and be aware of stepping in before they have finished. They will feel more engaged if they know that they have had a chance to make their point.

Dealing With Apathy

This can be hard, because you probably don't know the group well, and there may be reasons for apathy that have nothing to do with your workshop.

That said, it is still important to ensure that your activities are relevant, enjoyable, practical and clearly explained. This last point is very important, because a lot of energy can be lost, confusion created, and apathy developed when people are not clear about what they have to do.

A good way of ensuring success is to start the activity by visiting each group in turn, so that they can say back to you what they have to do, why they are doing it and what it will help them to achieve.

Scepticism – the Enemy of the Workshop

Dealing with scepticism is also difficult. The best way is to embrace it, and to be prepared to change plans accordingly if appropriate.

However, facilitators should also believe in what they are doing. Explain clearly why the work SHOULD help. Be prepared to listen to the comments from the group, but don't give up. This is yet another example of how flexibility is absolutely necessary.

Other Factors Which Can Lead To Things Going Wrong

There are many of these, latecomers (stress the importance of punctuality and have a cup of coffee ready to start the session), jetlag of participants (have energetic games at hands) and so forth.

However, remember the golden rules of being a facilitator. Be prepared, listen and get the group active. Do these things, and all will be well. Usually!

DAY WRAP UPS AND WORKSHOP CLOSING

Sadly, the day is coming to an end. Your aims have been met, your goals have been achieved, and fun has been had by all. But you still have another step before you wrap things up. The best facilitators are constantly reviewing their work.

Feedback where time has been available for reflection is the best, although that is not always possible to get. Therefore, make sure that your sessions end with a chance for a final reflection and some feedback.

A good way of doing this is by creating your own association cards. These are cards with emotions or feelings displayed through images. People are often happier, particularly the more reticent ones, to show their feedback this way, rather than through words. There are commercial products that can be adapted. Dixit cards, for example, are a part of a story telling game, but they can easily be employed to help with this part of the feedback questions.

Ask the group questions, some examples are below, and get them to pick a card that best shows their feelings towards these questions.

Such questions could include:
- How do you (i.e., the participant) feel after the workshop?
- What about the progress the group made as a team?
- How do you feel about what you will take away from the day?

The cards can then be the basis of a group discussion. The group can form a circle, and you can lead them round to offer the reasons for their choice of cards.

The next step can be the hardest. Here, you will ask the group to offer some feedback about you, as facilitator.

It is important to be open minded about the feedback you will receive. Sometimes, for some people, sessions will not live up to their expectations. Sometimes, we all can have a bad day. When criticism is offered, let the participants say whatever is on their minds.

Having said that, do word your request for feedback carefully. Crowd mentality can soon develop, and people feel caught up in the need to criticize, or, indeed to praise effusively without due consideration. Over-praise, like over-criticism, isn't very helpful. Just as a bit of criticism is good to receive, constant praise is nice, but does not help people to improve.

A good way of wording your request for feedback would be to say something like – 'Can you provide me with some constructive comments about my own work today, and, if you can, highlight the things that went really well?'

One of the final acts is to gain some written feedback. Print off some sheets such as the suggestion below and distribute them. Ask your group to fold them in half, to maintain privacy, since that will mean you receive more honest answers.

Workshop Survey	Strongly Disagree	Disagree	Agree	Strongly Agree
The objectives of the workshop were clearly defined.				
Participation and interaction were encouraged.				
The topics covered were relevant to me.				
The content was organized and easy to follow.				
This workshop experience will be useful in my work.				
The facilitator was well prepared.				
The workshop objectives were met.				
The time allocated for the workshop was sufficient.				
The meeting room and facilities were adequate and comfortable.				
The games were helpful to be energized and creative for the workshops.				
The workshop was fun.				

Trust the feedback, and act on it. This will help you on your journey to becoming the best workshop facilitator you can be.

The Last Game of the Book
Finally I would like to show you another game in which the participants can create a nice souvenir.

Ask them to draw a shield of 5 different categories and draw symbols for each category. After they have finished, they could put the drawings on a whiteboard and could discuss why they drew those symbols.

FOLLOWING UP

The workshop has gone brilliantly, you are happy, the participants are happy. They are off to the local bar, grateful to be finishing an hour earlier than on a normal day, and they invite you along. But, you've a commute ahead and there isn't time.

The first ten minutes your group, unbeknown to you, talk about what they've learned, how they will implement it.

Then the topic turns to TV and football, and the whole becomes divided.

Still, they are happy. Next day they get to work, but there is some catching up to do from their time away from the office. Then the weekend hits and by Monday their learning is a pleasant, but distant memory. How sad.

With an effective follow up to your delivery, however, you reduce the chances of the above happening.

Here are some ideas that help to ensure the learning of the workshop turns into practice in the workplace.

Planning your Follow Up
This should be a part of your initial planning. Also, share with the participants, and the people who hired you, that you will be doing this. It will inspire confidence, demonstrate your professionalism and tell your participants that the day, though packed with fun, will also lead to serious points being made.

This means that you, the facilitator, will need to block time in your diary to do this. Aim for three to six months from the date of the workshop, which should give time for the impact of the workshop to be evident.

Careful planning means that you should be able to follow up five to eight workshops in a day. Therefore, you probably (depending on how busy get) need to prepare for one or two days a month which will be follow up days.

Handouts

Ask your group to read through the handouts at some point in the next couple of weeks, while the workshop is still fresh in their minds. This will help to reinforce the points that were investigated. I would suggest to digitize every picture taken on the workshop (whiteboards, flipcharts) and send it to the participants. You could also ask the office manager to put a set of the handouts up in a lunch room or a corridor. Ask your participants to develop an action plan. This means that they will take a small number of the points from the workshop and work out a way to implement them. Thinking back to the chapter on small groups, where action plans with milestones were worked out, remind the group to make sure that the action plans have been implemented.

A great tool for the team to track progress is Trello (https://trello.com). Trello's boards, lists, and cards enable them to organize and prioritize their projects in a fun, flexible and rewarding way. And it's free. I usually use the following columns:

ToDo	Prioritized	In Progress	Blocked	Done	Parking Lot
Action items from the workshop	Action items which are ready to start	Action items in progress	Action items blocked usually because of external dependancy	It's clear, right? :)	Action items which are not that relevant or important at the moment.

Make an Idea Bank

If everybody does this, then there can be huge benefit to the company. The managers could even create a little bit of time, say half an hour per person, to produce this.

An idea bank can work as follows:

- Get your participants to work through their notes and any handouts within a couple of weeks of the workshop.
- Make three headings, and populate each with two or three ideas.
- First heading is for things you can teach to other workers at your business.
- Second heading is for ideas to improve the participants' own performances.
- Finally, the third heading is for your participants' own interests, and includes ideas about which they would like to learn more.

Send a Follow Up Email

Contacting participants and perhaps the managers who hired you for the workshop is valuable for a number of reasons. When contacting, you should focus on the impact of your sessions on the work and productivity of the business and the workshop employees.

- It gives a chance for you to troubleshoot difficulties.
- It reminds the participants of the session.
- It demonstrates that you, as the facilitator, are still interested in the outcomes of your session. This can be great publicity for you, and can earn you word of mouth recommendations.
- It gives you feedback. You can see what has really worked in terms of the impact made, and what needs re-working.

Use Social Media, or Other Online Media

This can be a great way of keeping in touch with your participants. It is a brilliant way of getting honest feedback. Certainly, get your attendees to complete feedback forms, but these are of limited value. Using social media is also a superb way of getting your name as a facilitator spread.

Make Use of the Workshop as a Starting Point

Tell your group that there will have been two major outputs from their workshop. Firstly, it will be what the group has gained as a whole. In other words, what they have learned as they sought to address the goals listed at the outset of the sessions.

And secondly, and this is just as important, each participant will have learned something unique to them. Express this idea to them and really drive it home. You might even get some contributions back from the attendees. This would be very useful, as the attendees will have found out aspects of their work that they really enjoy, bits that they don't like as much, things that they had not thought about before, strengths that were perhaps undiscovered and weaknesses which could be impacting on their performances at work.

For example, people working in the finance department might have discovered an unknown talent for selling their ideas. Someone in the administration staff might have unfound talents in tech. They should use these personal discoveries to explore, develop and learn. It will help them become better at their own jobs, and help their business to thrive.

By this point in the book, you will hopefully be clear that there are three parts to giving a workshop, and each are as important as the others.

Firstly, there is **PREPARATION** – planning for the workshop.

Next comes **DELIVERY** – the workshop itself.

Finally, there is the topic of this chapter – **FOLLOW UP**. Not only will the follow up assist participants in turning the findings of their workshop into benefits for their work, but it will also help you, as facilitator, to improve your own future workshops.

FINAL THOUGHTS

I hope you have found this book useful as you start and develop your role as a workshop facilitator.

You have learned, in the first chapter, the importance of workshopping, including from the perspective of the people who will become your clients. If your clients understand the power of this form of training and business development, not only will their company thrive, but they will become return customers.

You have learned of the importance of careful, detailed, and yet flexible planning. Without that, even the most experienced of workers will struggle to maintain focus on achieving goals. Remember, draw up a timetable. You can adapt it as you go along (indeed, you probably should) but you need that framework to be a success.

You should have an understanding of the importance of laying down rules, in a friendly and polite way, and using fun ice breakers to get people in the mood for work. You have some examples of these, but soon you will be creating your own, or adapting ideas that work well for you.

You have learned the importance of setting clear goals, either ones imposed on the workshop, or those collaboratively agreed upon by the group. And, you now know how to work with the group to achieve these.

In the chapters on small group and large group discussions, you have a plan of how to make these 'guts' of the workshop effective. And how to ensure that all can take part.

Hopefully, you will be clearer on theories of learning, and the importance of getting participants active and involved in their learning.

All workshops will have moments where things are not as lively as others. The post lunch period is often one of these, when the group has relaxed a little, and need their drive re-energized. Several games and activities have been suggested to get the group going again, and it is important to recap that good planning. Lively activities and adherence to effective learning styles will reduce the chances of these lapses occurring.

You should have some strategies to deal with recalcitrant attendees, the over enthusiastic, the unsure and the wary. Workshopping is a great way of being totally inclusive, because everybody can participate to the level at which they are comfortable.

You will now understand the importance of following up your workshop, and of getting back in contact with participants and clients to see how things worked out in practice. And we looked at ways in which feedback can be gained to help you become an even better facilitator.

Trust yourself. Plan carefully, keep up the pace, be in control and get feedback. Do those things and your workshops will be successful. Being a workshop facilitator is a great career. What's more, it's a chance to help people in their work and careers, and to assist the businesses that employ them, and to do so in a lively, interesting and fun way.

Made in the USA
Columbia, SC
08 January 2019